signed by author.   EKenBottwid
                                     £ 4 - 50

D1356462

SWALLOWS

Swallows flying above a chalk stream. The adult male above is distinguished from the female by the much longer forked tail. The young bird flying below is less strongly coloured and has a shorter tail.

PETER TATE

SWALLOWS

Illustrations by Alan Harris

Peter Tate

H. F. & G. WITHERBY LTD

TO MY FATHER

First published in 1981 by
H. F. & G. WITHERBY LTD
5 Plantain Place, Crosby Row,
London, SE1 1YN

© Peter Tate, 1981
ISBN 0 85493 140 6

Filmset in Monophoto 12pt Apollo
and printed in Great Britain by
BAS Printers Ltd
Over Wallop, Hampshire

INTRODUCTION

I have loved the swallow since I was a child. My earliest bird memories are of swallows twittering early in the morning outside my bedroom and swooping in and out of the stables all day long. I can still remember how sad I was when they assembled in September before they set off on their journey to Africa and how I longed to accompany them. They remain my favourite bird, and if this book helps others to love and rejoice in their beauty it will have served its purpose.

The European swallow and the Barn swallow of North America are sub-species, or races, of a single species, and I have treated them as such, for the differences in their life histories are tiny. The races from Asia and North Africa differ from them mainly in the colour of their underparts and also slightly in size. However the Egyptian race does not migrate and as such is set apart from the others, all of which make long migratory journeys to and from their breeding areas.

This book about the swallow, its life and legend, is not a detailed scientific monograph, and tables, statistics and graphs have deliberately been avoided. However I have tried to discuss and describe the bird as comprehensively as possible, and this has involved using the work of many people from many countries. The book is intended for all those who see and admire swallows and wish to know more about them, even though they may not be in any way serious ornithologists.

Peter Tate
Rickmansworth
April 1980

CONTENTS

COLOUR PLATES

BREEDING AND BEHAVIOUR

The swallow is familiar to everyone, even to those who have only the slightest interest in birds. Its beauty, the grace of its low, sweeping flight over meadows and streams and its soft twittering song all call to mind a peaceful, unchanging countryside. Throughout five continents it is favoured as a friend of man. Nor is it only recently that it has found its special place in the hearts of man. As long ago as 1496 a decree was issued in Milan protecting it, centuries before any other bird was so treated, except for some birds of prey used in falconry.

The swallow is a beautiful bird with a dark metallic blue mantle and collar, deep red forehead and chin, and creamy white underparts terminating in a deeply forked tail with long streamers. Its flight is buoyant and dashing and it is incredibly agile, sweeping and swerving inches from the ground as it feeds on insects.

It is no accident that the swallow is so close to man. Without the numerous nesting sites provided by buildings, culverts and ledges, it would have to depend on natural ledges in caves, or crevices in cliffs and rocks and its numbers would almost certainly be fewer. Such evidence as we have suggests that the

11

swallow was scarcer before man changed the face of the
countryside, and recent research in Canada has shown
that the availability of nesting sites does indeed
influence the swallow population.

The swallow (*Hirundo rustica*) is generally distri-
buted in the British Isles, and is present in small
numbers as far north as Orkney and Shetland. The
British Trust for Ornithology's atlas of breeding birds
shows that swallows breed in no less than 96 per cent of
Great Britain and Ireland. Only a few nests are found
above 1500 feet, although on the continent nests
frequently occur at higher altitudes. It seems likely that
the total number of swallows breeding in Great Britain
has decreased over the last thirty to forty years. If this is
so, changes in farming methods that have reduced the

insect population, and hence the birds' food supply, are no doubt mainly responsible. From the swallow's point of view, greater hygiene is not a good thing, and modern concrete, asbestos-covered milking parlours and stores are not as suitable for nesting as were old stables and cattlesheds.

One important element in man's love of the swallow must be that it is a harbinger of spring and the brighter days to come, a sign that winter is past and that the countryside is about to stir. The first swallows to arrive are usually males, the females following close behind. If a male has previously bred, he will make his way almost at once to the nesting place he used the previous year; should that spot no longer exist he will stay in the immediate vicinity and await the arrival of his mate. If she does not return, as is often the case, he will start to look for a new mate. Young birds about to breed for the first time frequently return to within twenty miles of their birth-place, although some, especially females, disperse well beyond that distance.

The male bird chooses the nest site. He advertises the fact that he has discovered a suitable spot, and that he wants a companion to share it with him, by circling around at a height of about 150 feet, singing his twittering song at the same time. When he sees another swallow approaching, he swoops down to the entrance to the nest site; if the bird is an interested female, he will fly to the precise spot he has chosen for the nest. There he perches and makes pecking movements. If the female stays, he starts his courtship display. Circling the nest site is not always the prelude to full courtship display and may sometimes be a kind of dress rehearsal for it. Certainly such circling also takes place at other times well into the breeding cycle, and I have seen it in early September, when courtship must be long past.

Although the swallow is a common and confiding bird that will remain on its nest or fly to it even when human beings are quite near, little is known of the display that leads to copulation. Despite many hours of observation, I have only seen part of it, and I have never actually seen swallows mating. As a result I can do no better than quote that careful observer the Reverend P. H. T. Hartley, writing in *British Birds* in 1941.

'One bird was circling round below the nest with a curious very slow and wavering flight, making several turns on a track about one yard in diameter. It held its tail very widely spread, with legs dangling. After several turns had been made, the second bird of the pair fluttered down from the nest and made a similar wavering circle following the first. Then both birds flew out of the mill.'

On another occasion a different observer watched a swallow glide slowly past its mate, which was perched on a telegraph wire, and then climb away steeply with its tail widely spread. Some birds have been seen carrying out a form of display while perched, the male taking up a horizontal posture with his head stretched forward and his beak pointing straight forwards; the chestnut feathers of his forehead and chin were fluffed up, but the rest of his plumage was drawn in and sleek. In most cases, before the actual mating takes place, the male flies down to perch alongside the female, who solicits him by leaning forwards horizontally, holding her wings a little way from her body.

Swallows also engage in aerial chases; sometimes three birds are involved, though more often there are two. Such behaviour is usually the result of rivalry between males and is not a sexual chase. A rapid, twisting flight makes it difficult to identify the sex of two birds so similar as male and female swallows, but on the few occasions when I have been reasonably certain of their sex, they were both males.

The reasons for the ritualized form of display carried out by swallows, and indeed by all birds, are threefold. First, it advertises the fact that the male bird has established a nesting site and is anxious to find a female willing to share it with him. Second, it often serves to establish the sex of an approaching bird, for in birds in which there is virtually no visible differences between the sexes a bird's reaction to certain display acts will indicate its sex. Third, and most important, display provides the mutual stimulation necessary to bring both birds to the same level of sexual stimulation at the same time. Birds are able to breed only once a year, during certain fixed periods, and for the rest of the year their sex drive and reproductive organs are dormant. They only become physically capable of reproduction as the time for breeding approaches; in many cases, although probably not in that of swallows, a degree of mutual hostility, even to birds of the same species, must be overcome. This hostility arises because in many species the male establishes a territory from which he excludes all other birds of the same species except his eventual breeding partner. Within this area he will nest, raise his family and feed himself and his brood. The size and form of this territory varies greatly from species to species according to habitat and circumstances. In a habitat with a good supply of food and good nesting sites its actual area will be smaller than in a poorer habitat. Some birds, seabirds in particular, claim little or no territory except the immediate area of the nest, which they will defend from intruders; the area where they obtain their food, that is the sea and the air, are considered neutral ground, as it were.

Although the majority of swallows actually nest alone they are frequently close enough to other nesting pairs to be able to mob possible predators communally. Such communal mobbing takes place when a cat walks through a farmyard where several pairs of swallows have their nests. The birds swoop and dive at it and at times just avoid hitting it, continually repeating their 'tswee' mobbing call. Such neighbourly help is by way of being a bonus not a necessity, and it has been shown that pairs breeding alone do not have a lower success rate than those that nest in company with others.

Although swallows do not drive other birds from the vicinity of their nest, they do on occasions react very fiercely to other bird species, even mobbing some that could not possibly be a hazard, such as common sandpipers and black terns. Understandably, crows, jays and birds of prey are liable to be mobbed since in various ways they do pose a threat to swallows. Some observers have reported that swallows specially fear the hobby. In Europe the hobby is certainly the bird of

prey most likely to attack them, as it is both fast and manoeuvrable enough to take a swallow in flight. There is no evidence, however, that the swallow forms a major part of its diet, at least in Britain. I have seen a hobby take a swallow and pursue another unsuccessfully, but the birds in the vicinity did not appear to take any general evasive action, and although there was some rather half-hearted mobbing as the hobby flew away it could hardly be said that the swallows were terrified. When ringing swallows in Spain, Mr A. L. Pimm was mobbed as he removed the captured birds from the nets, their harsh 'chirruping' calls attracting other swallows. When a hobby was nearby the swallows used the same type of alarm call, but not when lesser kestrels, kites or other birds of prey that do not take swallows were present. From North America have come similar reports of swallows mobbing a variety of birds, some of which could not threaten them.

Normally swallows like to nest on a beam or ledge quite close to the roof, for although the nest itself is open at the top they prefer to have some kind of cover close above them. Sheds and farm outbuildings are popular, so long as a broken window or partly open door enables the bird to reach its nest, and in some districts they breed inside chimney stacks. Old-fashioned farm stables or cow byres are particularly suitable sites, since besides providing plenty of nesting ledges they are not too light and have a plentiful supply of flies. They tend to avoid nesting in towns and large villages, except for the outskirts.

Swallows build their nests of mud pellets which they form in their mouths to the shape of flat drops. These are placed in the nest while they are still wet with the pointed end downwards. Small pieces of grass and rootlets are worked in, and they have been seen taking horsehair from a barbed-wire fence to strengthen their nests. The inside cup is lined with feathers, usually caught in mid air.

Swallows seem to have a strong preference for white feathers in the lining of the nest. In an experiment Mr Alan Parker replaced white feathers with coloured ones, and each time the birds removed them, rather than accept coloured feathers. They eventually left the nest unlined.

One nest dissected in the United States contained $7\frac{1}{2}$ ounces of dried mud, 1635 rootlets over half an inch long, 139 white pine needles, 450 pieces of dried grass, ten chicken feathers, four pieces of wood, two human hairs, a piece of leaf, cotton and a tablespoonful of minute pieces of rootlets and grass. Occasionally nests are built in the thatch of a roof or in a crevice in a stone wall without mud pellets. On the Californian coast, nests made mainly of seaweed have been found.

Birds sometimes nest in unusual spots, and the swallow is no exception. Among the strange sites the swallow has chosen have been an old robin's nest, a shoe-box and a bowl on a shelf, even a beer mug and lampshades and brackets, some still in use. Once a hat hanging on a stable wall provided the site for three nests. The most macabre nest of all must be one found in the USA in the dried corpse of an owl. In the USSR swallows have attached their nests to the larger nests of birds of prey. Once or twice a nest built like a house martin's on the face of a wall has been found. Moving sites include a portable milking-machine in a Devon field, an old fishing-boat moored off Aberlady,

Scotland, and, more remarkable still, a train in British Columbia that the birds followed on its regular two-mile journey. One strange site that caught my imagination was on the pelmet over the window in a lady's bedroom: to shield themselves from the light above the dressing-table, the birds built a little screen of goose feathers on the rim of the nest. Swallows will only very rarely nest in trees. One exception was a shattered poplar on the battle-field of Flanders during the First World War that contained no less than twelve nests, the lowest about 10 feet above the ground. As virtually every building has been reduced to rubble, the birds were driven to unusual nesting places, including deserted dugouts, some below ground. Nests below ground have also occasionally been found in Cornish mineshafts and in cave mouths. At the other end of the scale one nest found in Minnesota was 107 feet up in an observation tower. The fact that the birds can fly through very small openings extends the range of suitable nest sites, and one hole regularly used measured as little as $2\frac{3}{4}$ inches by 2 inches.

To begin with, both sexes help to build the nest, although the female completes the final stages and lines the nest bowl alone. Between six and ten days are usually needed to complete it, although twelve days or even more may be required if materials are scarce or in wet weather, when the mud takes longer to dry. Very occasionally a pair or a single bird becomes confused and does not stop building when the nest is finished but continues to add to the structure. This happened in a quite extraordinary nest found in Liège in 1971 that was no less than 185 cm long, 70 mm high and 80 mm deep. A continuous structure lying along the flange of a steel girder, it was used by two pairs of birds, although it is not clear whether all four birds worked on it together. In North America several examples have been found of swallows and flycatchers using and adapting each other's nests, mainly those sited beneath bridges. In one place there were seven alternating nests, one on top of each other rather like a layer cake, starting with a swallow's nest at the bottom of this remarkable edifice. Certainly in Mississippi, swallows have frequently chosen to build beneath short, wide bridges, often close to wasps' nests.

Most building activity takes place early in the day, and as the day progresses work drops off. This is almost certainly so as to allow the mud pellets to adhere properly and harden, as over-rapid construction often results in the collapse of the nests. In a dry situation a nest may last for several years; one at my home in Suffolk was used for three years with virtually no repairs, and no doubt many nests last still longer.

Considerable effort is needed to build even a simple nest. One intensive study made by a group of British prisoners-of-war in Bavaria in 1943 and 1944 revealed that the birds made twenty-eight visits an hour to the nests between 6 and 8 a.m. and as few as five an hour between 6 and 9 p.m. At a nest in the USA no less than 1200 visits were made during construction. Such detailed studies have helped to build up a picture of how birds live. Frequently a great deal of detailed observation is involved, quite often of small samples that may not be truly representative of the species as a whole. However, the result of a really detailed examination may be to make numerous tiny pieces of observation, apparently insignificant on their own, fit neatly into the overall life pattern of the species.

In the south of England, the laying season lasts from the end of April to the end of August, reaching a peak between 13 May and 16 June and a second, smaller one between 1 July and 21 July. In the north of England and Scotland the dates are about a week later. The variation from year to year is quite small, except in a very few years when the weather is quite abnormal.

Once the nest is complete, it is not long—usually four or five days—before the first egg is laid. The female lays a single egg in the morning on successive days. The normal clutch is four or five (the average number is in fact 4.4); clutches of six eggs are not unusual, and as many as eight have been recorded. The second clutch is smaller, averaging 3.8. Late broods laid in about the third week of August number well below four. As in many species, swallows nesting in the northern part of their breeding area tend on average to have larger clutches than those further south. Although the summer days are longer in the north, so giving more time to find food for the young, the short summer season there means that there is not enough time to raise second or third broods; hence the first and only brood is of great importance and must be as large as possible. In Great Britain, however, second broods are usual at least as far north as Banff in Scotland, and third broods are common. One remarkably late brood was recorded in 1899 by Miller Christy, at Walton-on-Naze, Essex, who found eggs being incubated in mid-December, but the chances of the nestlings surviving must have been remote indeed.

There is a conflict of evidence about whether incubation starts as soon as the first egg is laid. Observations made by the prisoners-of-war in Bavaria suggest that it does, whereas other ornithologists, myself among them, believe that it only begins when the clutch is complete.

The majority of swallows use a second nest for the second brood, although often a pair will chose an old unoccupied nest rather than build a completely new one. The change of nests probably takes place because a great many parasites, mainly lice, collect in the nest while the brood is being reared. One study in the Netherlands showed that as many as 19 to 20 per cent of birds may become infected by these bloodsucking insects, and that young birds are the worst affected. The parasites do not appear to harm the birds significantly, however.

The female is almost entirely responsible for incubation, and although the male undoubtedly does sit, he does so for short periods only. Some observers have suggested that the male takes a major part in incubation, but such variations seem to be a result of individual behaviour rather than changing patterns over the bird's range. During incubation, the temperature inside the eggs must be maintained as nearly as possible at 95.5 degrees Fahrenheit. The eggs are fully incubated by the sitting bird for approximately 70 per cent of daylight hours, with frequent short breaks to allow her to feed. During the hours of darkness the female seems to sit virtually all the time. The actual time spent on the eggs increases during the first week, tends to fall during the second week, only to increase once more as the time for hatching approaches.

Incubation lasts fourteen to sixteen days, the average being 15.3 days. Once the eggs have hatched, the nestlings are brooded mainly by the female, although the male may take a turn when they first hatch. The nestlings, which are almost devoid of down, have bright yellow mouth linings and edges to their bills; their eyes are closed. Brooding takes place during some 65 per cent of daylight hours and throughout the night. The amount of time during which the young are brooded steadily decreases as they grow and their covering of down and feathers develops. By the ninth day after hatching they are covered for only about 6 to 7 per cent of daylight hours, and soon after that they only need to be kept warm at night. Indeed, when the nestlings are almost fully grown, it is physically impossible for a parent to brood them, as anyone will know who has investigated a swallow's nest at night and has seen four or five pairs of eyes shining down.

The time the young birds spend in the nest between hatching and flight varies from seventeen to twenty-four days according to the weather and hence the availability of food. The nestlings require a great deal of food to sustain the substantial growth they achieve while in the nest, and catching this food makes a great deal of work for the adult birds. At one nest in Bavaria a brood of four young swallows received about eleven visits an hour from an adult carrying food during the first day; this had risen to about fifty visits an hour by the fourteenth day, although thereafter the number of feeding trips tapered off. At another nest the figures

were eighteen visits an hour on the first day and fifty an hour on the tenth. Both adult birds feed the nestlings; the number of visits they make is governed by the weather and by the particular character of the habitat in which the nest is situated. An old farmyard with a manure heap and warm weather both make the parent birds' task much lighter, whereas modern farm hygiene has brought increased work. The number of visits varies from place to place and season to season quite considerably. After leaving the nest the fledglings are fed by their parents for a while, usually on a perch, although occasionally both birds hover in the air while the food is passed over.

The nestlings gain weight rapidly. From some 2.5 grams at hatching they reach a peak of about 20 grams on the twelfth day, then drop to about 16 grams on the twentieth day, when they are usually ready to leave the nest. Their body temperature also increases from about 96 degrees Fahrenheit to 104 degrees when they leave the nest. The young are able to regulate their body temperature fully only some time after maximum weight is attained. As with many species whose young are born helpless, the nestling's maximum body temperature is not reached until it is ready to leave the nest. This reduces the problem of food supply a little, since more food is needed to achieve higher temperatures; it also means that while they are in the nest the young do not have to be at a peak of bodily activity and so can conserve their energy for growth and development.

In a few cases in both Europe and North America young swallows have been seen helping their parents to feed the nestlings of later broods; they have also been observed assisting in the building of a second nest. In one exceptional case worth mentioning a house martin was seen to feed young swallows. Such behaviour is not unknown in other species of birds; if an adult bird carrying food for its own brood sees a nestling intensely begging for food, it will sometimes feed it although it belongs to another species.

Swallows are opportunists when it comes to obtaining food for their young and for themselves, and they capture a very great variety of insects. It is usually quite impossible to identify the small insect food swallows take, and much of our evidence comes from detailed microscopic examination of faeces obtained near nests. A paper produced by members of the Department of Entomology at the Natural History Museum lists some sixty-three species of prey from many families, including aphids, beetles, moths, bees, wasps, craneflies, soldier flies, damselflies, hoverflies, house and blowflies. On one occasion an observer watched common wasps being brought in by the parent birds. When offered them, the nestlings did not seem to be very enthusiastic. Although their parents made no attempt to remove the stings, the nestlings showed no signs of being stung.

Along with martins and swifts, swallows are probably the smallest birds capable of gliding flight, which is such an important aid to feeding on the wing. When gliding a bird can accurately judge its precise position in relation to its prey, and a short, smooth glide to capture the insect is all that is necessary. In flapping flight, by contrast, a bird to a greater or lesser extent rises and falls with each wing beat. Films of flying geese or flamingoes demonstrate this, though admittedly in a somewhat extreme form; the bird has to flex its neck in order to keep its head and eyes on a steady path and counteract the body movement produced by its wing beats. The internal construction of the swallow's eyes assists it considerably in feeding, and its good forward binocular vision is essential in judging distance accurately. In comparison with those of many small birds, the swallow's eyes are inclined to the front of its head, though they are not as forward-looking as those of owls or eagles. Swallows' eyes have two specially sensitive areas of the retina, called fovea. One provides all-round normal vision; the second gives forward binocular vision, a characteristic swallows share with hawks, eagles and humming-birds, all of whom must be able to judge distance accurately.

The swallow's ability to manoeuvre in flight is also helped by its low wing loading. This, at 14.3 grams per 100 square centimetres of wing, is much lower than most bird species. Its wing beat, about four to the second, is much slower than that of the swift, (about ten per second), which feeds in a similar way.

Swallows tend to feed in the air at lower levels than house martins and sand martins, which use the middle region of the air, and swifts, which usually feed high in the air. Swallows swoop low over the fields and woods in search of food, sweeping up to clear hedges, bushes and fences and then dropping back again. They often gather in fields where cattle are feeding and take the flies that follow the animals and those that are disturbed by the cattle's feet. They were seen following soldiers in the Libyan desert and catching the insects their feet disturbed, and they have even been observed associating with starlings feeding on the ground. In Africa grass fires attract huge numbers of swallows of several different species, including the European swallows, which feed on the insects trying to escape from the flames. Some authorities have also suggested that swallows are attracted to fires because they like to 'smoke bathe', a theory supported by the fact that swallows flock to garden bonfires. It has been noted that several species of birds like to sit in smoke perhaps from a chimney. This may be a way of killing off feather parasites. However it could be that they are interested in the large number of insects disturbed by the bonfire rather than in the fire itself.

In difficult feeding conditions, bad weather for instance, swallows resort to a number of unusual methods. While they are on the ground they may occasionally take insects or torpid flies from thistles, and they have even been seen to take caterpillars from tree foliage, hovering around the tree with much wing-fluttering. Unusual feeding habits are not always successful and swallows have been trapped in sewage sludge and in the mud of the Ribble estuary in Lancashire while searching for insects. They have also taken flies attracted to rotting seaweed on a beach and froghoppers from a reservoir. *In extremis* they have even been known to take bread put out for sparrows, and decaying vegetable matter. In calm weather some swallows have been seen to take insect life of some sort from the surface of the sea.

Swallows drink by flying very low over the surface of a pool or stream, dipping their lower mandible into the water and scooping up a mouthful of liquid. they continue doing this until their thirst is satisfied. They bathe in a similar way, plunging right into the water with a splash and then emerging in a shower of spray several times in succession.

Swallows have been seen to dust-bathe, although this is rather unusual: Colin Tubbs once watched no less than fourteen swallows dust-bathing on a patch of cinders on a cart track in Hampshire. Swallows also occasionally take a bath in heavy dew on grass and have been known to bathe in the spray at Victoria Falls, Zambia. There is also at least one record of a swallow swimming; during ringing operations beside a lake in Zimbabwe one fell into the water and swam some 10 feet or so to the reeds, adopting a kind of butterfly stroke with its wings. A very similar incident was reported from the river Eden near Carlisle when a bird hit the water and swam to the bank.

*   *   *   *

Bird songs and calls are extremely difficult to describe, and those of the swallow are no exception. The main, or primary song, which most people will recognize, is a cheerful twittering ending in a rather wheezy trill. It is often uttered in flight but is almost as frequently sung from a perch such as a telephone wire or a dead twig, though rarely from a leafy bough. It is not as full or beautiful a song as that of the nightingale or blackbird, but its happy spontaneous quality is most warm and endearing. The song is heard most often early in the day, least often late in the evening, though it may be heard at any time. Although there have been one or two accounts of an aerial dawn chorus of swallows, this kind of song display is, sad to say, rather unusual and few people have had the good fortune to hear it. One witness near Liège in August-September saw a number of birds climb high into the sky before dawn and begin to sing. As the light became brighter they gradually descended, the strength of the song decreasing, as they swooped lower and flew faster.

Swallows continue to sing throughout the summer, and often a male will sing from a perch near the nest quite late in the breeding season. On a number of occasions in August I have heard a group of about thirty swallows singing and twittering together, both during short flights and while perched, though never in a high dawn flight. At such a late stage in the breeding season, this communal singing cannot be related to breeding in any way. Singing from the ground may occur more often than rare reports of it suggest.

On the whole, the primary song is associated with breeding and display. Unlike some species, however, swallows sing both on the wing and from a perch near the nest throughout the summer. Like other birds, the swallow has a number of specific calls that convey a particular message; these are in effect a kind of bird language. Whereas in some species such as the great tit or chaffinch that have been studied a great deal quite a vocabulary of calls and songs can be identified, the number of recognizable swallow's calls is not very great. The mobbing call that serves mainly to alert other birds to the presence of a possible predator is a staccato high-pitched 'tswee' repeated several times, usually as the bird dives. When nearing the nest, parent birds of both sexes announce their arrival to the nestlings with a sharp 'tschwick' call. Birds in flight quite often emit a 'tswik' call; this may be to maintain contact between birds feeding or travelling, away from the nesting place.

*　　*　　*　　*

The greatest error when considering the behaviour of birds is to attempt to interpret it in human terms. Birds live their lives by a fairly simple set of rules. When one activity finishes, another begins, usually in a set order: when the nest is complete, the eggs are laid, and then they are incubated; when they hatch, the young are fed, and when they fledge and become independent many birds go back to square one and mate, and the process begins again. If something out of the usual sequence of events happens the bird may become confused and react in a quite irrelevant manner. For example, one swallow that always perched on a particular electricity wire became completely disorientated when the wire was removed, hovering and repeatedly trying to land where the wire had been. Similarly, swallows have been seen bringing food to an empty nest some time after the young had flown. Sometimes one pair of birds builds two nests. On one occasion in Tipperary two eggs were laid in each, and the birds tried to incubate the nests alternately, but the eggs chilled and both nests failed. Although such examples of unusual behaviour should not be given undue weight, they are not without interest and do demonstrate that a creature following a fixed, pre-planned course can be deflected in odd ways if events do not follow their normal course.

One strange piece of behaviour that seemed to be the result of a whole string of mixed reactions was recorded by Mr E. I. Cuthbertson. A pair of swallows had built a nest on a curtain rail in a bedroom at Sedburgh, Yorkshire. On 17 June the first egg was laid, and on the same day it was found broken on the floor some distance from the nest. Another egg was laid on 28 June and then another two. Incubation started, but on 3 July an adult swallow was found dead under the nest. Until 5 July only one bird was seen, but then two birds visited the nest together. One of them began to build up the nest rim despite the efforts of the sitting bird to prevent it, and eventually the nest reached some 3 inches deep. The three eggs it contained hatched on 15 July. The next morning an adult swallow was seen carrying a nestling out of the window, and a little later another nestling was found on the floor. By the evening of 16 July the nest was empty. This entire episode is completely at variance with the bird's normal behaviour, and a rational explanation is very hard to find, although a conflict of behaviour was obviously involved.

Although there is considerable dispute among students of bird behaviour as to whether birds engage in 'play', there are a number of actions that I believe can only be adequately described as such. For example, a swallow has been seen to pick up a loose feather and let it fall and then swoop and catch it again in mid-air, repeating the process for quite a few minutes. The bird in question was an adult, so this was not a case of play being used to teach young birds to catch aerial prey.

On occasions swallows have been known to adapt their feeding behaviour to suit changed circumstances, an indication that they are not entirely 'programmed', to use current jargon. Swallows were once feeding at 4.0 a.m. on insects attracted to neon street lamps, and Derek Goodwin has described one incident when an extremely hungry young swallow entered an army tent in Libya and begged as it would to its parents before whichever soldier was holding the tent's flyswatter. In a rather similar way, a young swallow that had been found wet and exhausted in Lincolnshire and had been taken into a car to be dried and to recover from its ordeal took flies from the windscreen rather like a chameleon while being held by its rescuer. Sadly it did not survive and died a short while later.

The swallow is not a particularly aggressive bird, but nevertheless individuals can be distinctly vicious. It has for instance been known to evict a spotted flycatcher from its nest and then raise its own brood there. Swallows have even evicted a pair of robins, and there is some evidence that they then killed the young robins and forced the robins out when they made a second attempt at nesting. Such viciousness is entirely out of character, but no doubt there are psychopaths among birds just as there are among men. Swallows themselves are sometimes evicted by extremely aggressive species such as starlings and house sparrows. In the USA evictions by house wrens, which also puncture the swallows' eggs, have been reported.

Swallows have been observed pursuing pipistrelle bats hawking for insects at dusk, and I have seen a male swallow harry a bat in broad daylight in the middle of an August afternoon. Although the attacks were clearly deliberate, they were not pushed home, and the bat was not actually struck.

The swallow is not normally a victim of the cuckoo, probably because it almost always builds its nests indoors. Nevertheless several exceptions have been recorded, although for a cuckoo to enter a building to find a swallow's nest and then to lay its egg in such cramped condition does seem out of character. One incident in Staffordshire in 1972 is worth recounting in some detail. Several swallows nested in an open-ended shed with wooden roof beams beneath an asbestos roof. The edge of the nest was only about $1\frac{1}{2}$ inches below the roof, a gap quite sufficient for a swallow but so remarkably tight a fit for a cuckoo that it is thought it had to hover when placing its egg in the nest. Although it is now well established that cuckoos lay directly into their host's nest, this particular site must have posed considerable problems. A similar case occurred in Somerset in 1951, when a cuckoo was found to have laid in a swallow's nest inside a brick stable. The young cuckoo successfully fledged and was not only fed by the swallow foster parents but also by a pair of hedge sparrows who on several occasions were deflected from feeding their own brood by the loud and incessant cries of the baby cuckoo. In North America the swallow is occasionally parasitised by the cowbird.

*   *   *   *

Starvation encountered on migration accounts probably for most swallow deaths, far more than does old age. Such deaths tend to pass unnoticed except in a major disaster when literally thousands of birds are found dead. Few avian predators are capable of taking swallows, except the hobby and Eleonora's falcon, and the number taken by these forms a minute percentage of total deaths. A woodchat shrike was once seen to kill a swallow, but this was under abnormal circumstances, when both were resting on board a ship. Remains of swallows have been found on several occasions in the pellets regurgitated by owls. In a very unusual incident recorded in Hungary, house sparrows ate nestling swallows killed by cold; having developed a taste for such food, the sparrows went on to kill and eat the second brood.

Although the bird is such a superb and agile flyer, a few swallows die after colliding with objects such as power cables, and considerable numbers are killed when they hit road traffic. Perhaps one of the strangest deaths was when a swallow was killed in 1888 by a cricket ball at Felstead School, and to a slow underarm delivery at that! One or two birds have been killed by golf balls in both Europe and the USA. Juvenile birds have been found dead entangled in brambles, and one was trapped in sheep's wool hanging from a barbed wire fence, although this bird was lucky enough to be released alive. One can hardly think that a swallow might fall victim of a fish, but at least one case is known, at Ndumu in Natal, where a tigerfish took and ate a low-flying swallow as it swooped over a lake. Such deaths may not be quite as unusual as they seem, given the bird's habit of flying so low as to touch the water; a predatory fish would have no problem taking the bird. The most extraordinary and unexpected death must be that met by one unfortunate individual in Massachusetts, who was caught and swallowed by an enormous bullfrog. Another strange though not fatal accident occurred in Waterford, when a bird took and was caught by a fly hanging from a fisherman's line; it was released none the worse for its impetuousness.

It is difficult to estimate the age of mortality of any wild bird, especially as less than one in a hundred ringed swallows are ever recovered. However it is possible to calculate a reasonably accurate figure, since we know that average mortality is about 63 per cent and that probably half the birds that leave for their winter quarters each autumn will not return the following spring. The oldest known swallow lived till it was sixteen, but there is a great difference between the age which an individual may reach and the age at which the majority of the species die. Fully mature birds have a greater life expectancy than do juveniles. Even small non-migratory birds such as tits suffer a huge mortality in the early months of life, and swallows and similar birds have in addition to face the enormous challenge of a 12,000-mile return journey, some third of it across one of the largest and harshest deserts in the world. We do not know the percentage of swallows that die during the long migration, but it must be very high.

MIGRATION

For me there are few more enjoyable experiences than seeing my first swallow of the year, even if it is only a brief flash of deep metallic blue and an impression of grace and beauty as the bird flies low on its way to its summer home. A swallow on migration somehow seems to have a more determined and steadfast appearance than when it is simply flying about during normal daily feeding. Although it may swerve to take a passing insect, the whole impression is one of urgency, especially in the spring, when the need to breed drives it on; in autumn its actions seem to be rather more leisurely. The first swallows of the year are not only a sign of the coming summer. What excites the imagination just as much is the realization that this bird, weighing less than an ounce, is completing a journey that has taken it more than twelve thousand miles since it left its nest the previous autumn.

This pattern of departure and return has excited wonder and interest since the earliest times. In Ancient Greece the poet Anacreon and Aristotle both referred to swallows and their comings and goings, as did the elder Pliny in classical Rome. They were chiefly interested in the possibility that the birds hibernated, although Anacreon held to the theory of migration as a result of his observations. He is the first person of whom we know to believe that the birds flew to warmer climes to escape the cold of winter. However, theories of hibernation held sway until the end of the eighteenth century. It was even suggested that some flew to the moon for the winter. One such belief was that swallows, and other birds such as house martins and swifts, spent the winter buried in the mud at the bottom of ponds and lakes. Although it was not universally accepted, this idea is perhaps not entirely unreasonable, given the state of knowledge before systematic observations and records began to be kept. Especially when they gather in early autumn before migration, swallows often roost in reed-beds at night; hence it is not entirely surprising that people should have deduced, when they saw them no more, that they had crept down into the mud until the warmer weather would return. Several writers, among them Linnaeus, and Daines Barrington, with whom Gilbert White corresponded for many years, were convinced that swallows hibernated. Pontoppidan, the Norwegian naturalist recounted stories of fishermen who had netted birds which, once warmed, flew around the boats. Additional evidence for the hibernation theory was provided by the fact that, on their return in spring swallows were often seen feeding over or close to water. It was not appreciated that their insect food was not always available at that time over the fields.

In some respects swallows are not very robust, and in cold weather when they have been unable to feed adequately, a group may sometimes cluster together in an attempt to conserve their body heat. In such conditions, a bird's body temperature may drop as much as 10 to 20 degrees Fahrenheit and this hypothermia soon causes near paralysis. This apparent sleepiness must have added further weight to the belief in hibernation, particularly as the birds soon become active when taken to a warm place, so long as they had not lost too much weight. Thus in 1750 Jacob Klein, a German naturalist, recounted that a bundle of swallows taken from a lake near Baltiysk in Russia and brought to a fire started to fly about. Although Klein investigated a number of cases in which swallows were reported to have been found under water, or even under ice, he never claimed to have witnessed the actual discovery of the birds or their subsequent revival himself.

It is all too easy and tempting to scorn those who believed that swallows hibernated. The birds' wintering areas in Africa remained unexplored and unknown until well into the nineteenth century, and no satisfactory means of marking individual birds such as by ringing had been invented, although in Germany during the eighteenth century J. L. Frisch is said to have tied threads dyed with water-colours to the legs of swallows: when the birds reappeared in spring with the colours still bright he argued that they could not have spent the winter under water.

It is perhaps worth mentioning at this point how unwise it is to regard even the most unlikely seeming events in nature as impossible. One discovery that threw entirely new light on what had previously been dismissed as ornithological legend was made in

December 1946 by an American E. C. Jaeger, when he found a Poorwill, a species of nightjar, in a deep rock crevice in a canyon in the Colorado desert. The bird was inert, no heart-beat or breathing could be detected, and its body temperature was some 40 degrees Fahrenheit, below normal for the species. Jaeger ringed the bird, which was then found in the same crevice in four successive winters. A second bird was discovered in a similar state. Although so far no others have been found, the country is so wild and rugged that there may well be a large number unseen. This discovery proved that some birds do hibernate, at least for a period, but whether only a tiny number or many do so is not known. Although we can be virtually certain that swallows do not hibernate, it would be unwise to be dogmatic about the point in all species.

During the Middle Ages and indeed the seventeenth century most works of zoology and ornithology were literal translations of books by Greek and Roman writers that simply repeated hearsay information and argument. It was only as a consequence of the gradual revolution in scientific thinking during the sixteenth and seventeenth centuries and the development of independent methods of observation that original ideas on topics such as migration evolved.

Among their foremost exponents were John Ray, one of the greatest all round British naturalists, and his friend Francis Willughby who together published *Ornithologia*, first in Latin in 1676 and then in English two years later. *Ornithologia* was one of the first true bird books and was vastly superior to all previous works, and indeed to many that followed it. Sir Thomas

Browne, a very able seventeenth century naturalist living in Norwich, was one of the first to argue for migration, at a time when the hibernation theory was still generally accepted. A century later William Arderon, also of Norwich, strongly advocated the migration theory too, whereas the great Gilbert White of Selborne never finally made up his mind. The observations of his brother, who lived in southern Spain, did lead him to think that at least some birds migrated, nevertheless he relates stories of birds found hibernating.

Thomas Foster writing in 1817 in a book with the splendid though somewhat daunting title *Observations of the Natural History of Swallows, with a collateral statement of facts relative to their migration and to their brumal torpidity*, came down firmly on the side of migration, although he did consider the other side of the argument. What most served to convince Foster were contemporary accounts of swallows caught on ships off Senegal in October, along with the fact that swallows were reported in that area in spring and autumn but never in summer. He also mentions other reports of the birds being seen flying south over the Mediterranean as additional evidence that the birds left Europe.

Not until the practice of ringing was established could the migration theory finally be proved. In 1899 the Danish naturalist H. C. Mortensen became the first person to use rings with a return address and a unique serial number, both of which are vital if accurate results are to be obtained. He ringed 164 starlings with light metal rings, most of which were found not far from his home. In England at about the same time Lord William Percy marked young woodcock on his estate at Alnwick, Northumberland, with an 'N' and the year.

The practice of marking, as distinct from ringing, is old established. In ancient Rome swallows were removed from their nestlings and taken to the stadium when chariot races were to be held. When the race was over, threads of the winner's colours were tied to the legs and the birds were released, thus bringing the racing results to watchers at the nest.

The first comprehensive programmes of ringing were started in 1909 by Harry Witherby and Arthur Landsborough Thomson. Landsborough Thomson's scheme was based at Aberdeen University and ceased during the First World War. Witherby's, which was organized from London in conjunction with the magazine *British Birds* came under the control of the British Trust for Ornithology in 1937, which now administers all ringing in the British Isles.

Recoveries made through ringing schemes all over the world have gradually built up information about the routes taken by migrating birds and their main wintering areas. As more and more recoveries are made, the picture becomes more detailed and also far more complex, and the unanswered questions ever more tantalising. While for instance we know the distance individual species migrate, we do not know why some birds go further than others. In some species juveniles and adults do not migrate, merely flying down from the mountains to the valleys. Some individual members of one particular species migrate whereas others do not; thus robins from the Netherlands migrate, whereas almost all of those from Great Britain stay in one place. One of the most important unanswered questions is how birds navigate over thousands of miles and return some months later not merely to the same area but to the same building in the same village. It now appears that no single method is used, and current investigations seem to suggest that a single bird may use a number of navigational clues and methods at the same time and that different species may not all use exactly the same methods. So far, research has concentrated on finches, warblers, some of the larger seabirds and, most important of all, pigeons.

Ringing returns accumulating over several decades have provided an indication of the general routes taken by migrating swallows, although the detailed picture is by no means clear. Swallows ringed in the British Isles spend their winter in western Natal and southern Cape Province in South Africa.

Most swallows leave southern Britain in late September or early October and reach Cape Province during November. A few, leaving in late October or early November, arrive in December. Some arrive as early as the end of August, having left at the end of July. These are probably birds that failed to breed at all, or the ones that did not go on to produce a second brood. A tiny number stay in south Africa during the southern winter, but there is no evidence of breeding there, as has been the case with a very small number of house martins and European bee-eaters. Recent evidence has shown swallows from Britain moving their winter quarters in Southern Africa further south and west, perhaps due to climatic changes.

The first recovery of a swallow ringed in Britain was in South Africa on 27 December 1911, and by the end of 1979 5,486 birds ringed in Britain had been recovered, in addition to a great many originating throughout Europe and in much of the USSR, even Siberia. A major difficulty in establishing exact routes is that on migration the birds pass through vast, thinly populated areas even more thinly covered by ornithologists. It is certainly a fact that the further north the swallow breeds, the further south it spends the winter. Thus there occurs a kind of leap-frogging action in which birds from Britain and the USSR travel further than those from Germany, which tend to travel to parts of Zaire. Birds that summer in southern Spain hardly cross the Equator at all.

The route swallows take from Britain follows a fairly clear path down the west coast of France, across the Pyrenees, along the east coast of Spain, over the Mediterranean into Morocco and thence across the Sahara. A few recoveries in autumn have been made in Ghana and the Ivory Coast, which suggests that at least some birds fly to the west of the direct line across the desert.

Once the great challenge of the Sahara has been overcome, the birds fly on across southern Nigeria and Cameroun, over Zaire, Angola, Namibia and so into South Africa. Some birds take a more easterly line from the Mediterranean and have been recovered in Tunisia, and a few have been found in Tanzania and Zambia. Birds from mainland Europe travel further east, a great many flying down the Nile valley into East Africa. On the return flight in spring, the birds follow broadly the same route.

Because of the lively and intensive interest of some ornithologists in South Africa, we have a much clearer picture of the movement of swallows there than elsewhere in Africa. Although vast numbers of swallows pass down the Nile Valley on their way to East Africa, the origins of the birds wintering there is uncertain. There is some evidence however that the population that breeds in the Black Sea region of the USSR, spends the winter in Uganda. A strange situation for which there is as yet no logical explanation is that the few recoveries of Dutch and Belgian birds that have been made are widely scattered across Africa.

As mentioned earlier swallows do not cover such huge distances without very heavy mortality, even though there are no long flights over sea. Fortunately, they are not generally shot and trapped for food except in Italy, in contrast to small warblers and thrushes, which are especially vulnerable in the Mediterranean region.

Since swallows feed on airborne insects as they fly, they do not have to fatten themselves up before migration anything like as much as some small warblers. Whitethroats for instance increase their weight by 60 per cent or more before they set off. In very wet and cold weather, however, when the supply of insects decreases or ceases altogether, swallows are rapidly affected by the food shortage. Some of the birds quickly become lethargic and begin to cluster together for warmth; after this unconsciousness quickly follows, the bird's temperature falling so much that its metabolism slows down dramatically. Swallows cannot survive in this state for more than a few hours, and on some occasions a large number have perished in this way. Fortunately, however, since only part of the population is ever affected at any one time, the species as a whole is not greatly reduced.

Tropical storms also kill huge numbers, a Belgian for instance reporting numerous deaths in a tornado at Upemba in Zaire. The most spectacular disasters, which have also attracted widespread public attention, are those when birds crossing the Alps have been trapped by early snow or prolonged torrential rain. In two such disasters rescue operations helped to save the migrating birds. In late September 1931 many thousands were flown over the Alps from Austria to Italy; at the same time of year in 1974 some 470,000 birds were flown or taken by train from Switzerland over the mountains into Italy. Well intentioned and planned as these mercy flights were, only a small percentage of the migrating birds were saved, and many of these proved too weak to recover and died soon after they were released.

It is not only over Europe that swallows are at risk from low temperatures. In January 1961, for instance, in the Bredasdorp district of southern Cape Province, South Africa, numerous swallows were found clustering together inside barns during a sudden cold spell, something they would do in their winter quarters only in the most exceptional circumstances, and many died. In England in autumn 1979 the press reported that swallows had hurled themselves at house windows in East Kent, apparently in an attempt to get inside out of the cold. Mass deaths are probably not at all infrequent, but most go unrecorded, especially those caused by tropical storms over the Sahara or in the wilder areas further south. In addition, many thousands of swallows die of starvation or exhaustion during the long journey. It is only when significant numbers are actually seen dead or dying that the great dangers the birds undergo during migration can be brought to public attention.

There is much more we would like to know about the life of the swallows, especially after they leave our shores. Although for instance we have identified the main wintering areas in South Africa, it may be that some birds spend the winter elsewhere. In West Africa in particular the picture is very unclear. A few birds do winter there, but we do not know where they come from; others pass through virtually without stopping, while yet others seem to linger for two or three months and then move on again to an unknown destination. We do not know how many birds use the different routes or even the precise routes they take. We know that many birds, including as we have seen, many from Britain, cross the Sahara desert, the most direct but most difficult route. Others follow the bulge of West Africa and spend some time in the humid forest areas of the Ivory Coast, Ghana and southern Nigeria, and that still others take a short cut across the Gulf of Guinea. But we do not know where each of these groups comes from or where they go. Nor do we know why birds from Germany, most of which is further south than Britain, should winter 1000 miles north of those from Britain. Did swallows' wintering areas differ at all when the Sahara was less wide than it is today and did swallows use different winter quarters when their population was smaller than it is now?

*   *   *   *

In their winter quarters, free from the ties of eggs and young, swallows tend to move about singly and in small flocks during the day, gathering in very large flocks before roosting at night. According to a reliable estimate, one winter roost in a small marsh only about 550 by 650 yards at Lake Chrissie in the Transvaal contained about one million birds. As they flew in and circled around before landing, the birds gave the appearance of a whirling cloud, which suddenly dropped into the reeds just as darkness was falling. In the morning the swallows left in two distinct waves, making what an observer described as 'an explosion of birds, a veritable breaker of swallows . . . washing overhead'. This magnificent spectacle was observed on 14 March 1954, a time when many migrants must have already begun their journey north. All the swallows at this roost that were actually identified were European, but it is possible that at least some of them were of other species, since several species do occur in the area.

At Rosherville Dam near Pretoria, another large reed-bed roost in the Transvaal, some tens of thousands of swallows have been ringed by members of the Witwatersrand Bird Club. This roost is smaller than the one at Lake Chrissie, but the ringing programme has already provided much valuable data on site loyalty, moult and weight. Even urban sites, such as the Melrose Dam in the suburbs of Johannesburg, may contain a roost of several thousand swallows. Although reed-beds are popular roosts, smaller ones have been situated in poplar trees and bullrushes, and in Thailand huge numbers roost on telegraph and electric wires in the centre of Bangkok. When roosting on wires, the birds space themselves evenly some inches apart. One explanation for this may be that a little space makes it easier to take wing in a hurry without hitting a neighbour, but in fact studies made in the USA have shown that the more likely reason is that birds will not allow another bird to approach within a given distance without becoming nervous and preparing to fly off. It is interesting to note that another individual of the same species will be tolerated closer than a member of another species.

*   *   *   *

A question often asked but hard to answer concerns the speed of migration. How long does it take a bird to fly over from South Africa to England? Unfortunately we do not know when a particular bird leaves on its migration flight and when that same bird arrives; nor do we know the exact distance flown. The best estimate we can give at the moment is based on a swallow ringed in Johannesburg and recovered 7500 miles away in the USSR thirty-four days later. It must have covered on average 210 miles a day at the absolute minimum, since it is unlikely that it was caught immediately on arrival.

As they fly low over the ground when feeding and swoop and swerve over meadows or a pond, swallows seem to be travelling very fast. If you ask someone how fast they think a swallow flies, they will suggest a speed of 50 or 60 mph. In fact their speed is much slower, as a number of experiments made in the USA with a sophisticated type of Doppler radar equipment, similar to that used by traffic police, have shown. In 243 observations made of a number of birds at a farm in Michigan under varying wind conditions, the mean speed was 17 mph when flying across the wind, 22.2 mph with the wind and 16.7 mph against the wind. The maximum speed recorded was 35 mph. These figures do indicate how easy it is to over estimate the speed of a small object such as a bird flying in a rather dashing manner close to the ground. There is the same tendency to over estimate the speed of low-flying aircraft in competitions; even experienced observers have made errors of as much as 100 per cent. Many estimates of the speed of swallows and other birds have been recorded by observers who were themselves in an aircraft or car moving more or less alongside a flying bird. In such circumstances the nearness of the bird, its angle of flight relative to the observer and the accuracy of the speedometer or watch used all determine the accuracy of the measurement. Indeed over a short distance a tiny error in timing with a stopwatch will lead to gross inaccuracy.

The speed with which a bird completes its migration is not directly connected with its normal flying speed, because it will not necessarily fly on a direct course and a swallow feeding as it flies will inevitably progress in a rather indirect manner. The theories propounded at the end of the last century about the speed of the migration flight are very interesting. In 1890 Heinrich Gätke, the great pioneer of migration studies and founder of the observatory at Heligoland, claimed that the bluethroat flew at no less than 180 mph and the American golden plover at over 200 mph. He also maintained that birds migrated at heights up to 40,000 feet. In these ideas Gätke was wildly wrong. He was considerably nearer the truth, however, when he argued that some small birds fly without stopping for very great distances, suggesting in particular that bluethroats fly non-stop from the Nile Delta to Heligoland. At the time the idea that any small bird could possibly fly so far without feeding and resting was dismissed as impossible. However, recent research has shown that many species of small migratory birds feed very heavily before starting to migrate and build up such large reserves of fat under their skin and in the body cavity that their 'normal' weight of twelve grams increases to twenty grams. This reserve of surplus fat supplies enough energy to enable the bird to fly for about 60 to 90 hours, enough for a journey from North Africa to Britain or across the Sahara. Since swallows are able to feed on aerial food during their journey, they do not build up such large fat reserves as small birds such as the sedge warblers. Like swallows, house martins and swifts feed *en route* and migrate by day when they can see their food, The small warblers, thrushes and pipits, which feed around vegetation, have by contrast to migrate in stages at night, feeding and building up their reserves at each stopping place.

The dates on which swallows arrive and depart vary widely in different parts of the country and also depend on weather conditions. Birds may arrive on the south coast two to four weeks before they reach northern Scotland. This pattern repeats itself in autumn, when birds which have nested in northern

Scotland may start to migrate south in late August, a full month before they finally leave British shores. In general terms, however, it can be said that swallows are present in numbers from mid-April until early October. A few arrive in mid-March, and a few stay until November, and there are even stragglers before and after those dates.

In a few exceptional cases birds do overwinter in Europe. One such bird was living apparently quite successfully in a large building in a steelworks in Northamptonshire, where the temperature remained high and there was presumably sufficient insect prey. Sadly the bird was killed by a cat at about Christmas. it would have been extremely interesting to know if it could have survived the winter in such an unusual habitat, for under normal conditions there would not be enough insects. Expert aviculturists such as Frank Meaden have succeeded in keeping hand-raised swallows taken from their nests through the winter in a large aviary on a diet of soft food such as minced dandelion, steamed, minced ox heart and liver and chopped mealworms and moth larvae. Whether a fully grown bird could live for long on such a diet is less certain, and certainly only a very experienced person would initiate an experiment of this kind.

In spring the northward journey across Europe takes some ninety-seven days. The swallows reach Gibraltar on about 13 February, and the main arrival in north Norway at Varanger is not until 21 May, although the advance guard may be considerably earlier. At first the birds move slowly across southern Europe, and the south of France is not reached until about 15 March.

Then they speed up, and by the beginning of April most of central France, Switzerland and southern Germany have welcomed the first swallows. By the second week of April they have reached southern England and also the whole of the Low Countries and Germany. It is the beginning of May before many arrive in northern Scotland and Denmark, but by the middle of that month they have reached Lapland and by June a very few touch the Arctic Ocean.

The birds' progress across the continent has been shown by H. N. Southern to correspond quite closely to the 48 degree Fahrenheit isotherm. This connection with temperature is reinforced by the fact that insect food is not available in any quantity until the air temperature is close to 50 degrees Fahrenheit. The milder climate on the Atlantic seaboard of Europe means that birds travel further north earlier in the west, than they do in central and eastern Europe and Asia.

In the American continent the birds winter in that part of South America between Colombia and Guiana and central Argentina and central Chile, although a few may remain in central America and a few may venture to the far south of the continent. In the spring they arrive in the far south and south-east of the USA in late February and reach the north by mid-May, but as in Europe they do not make constant progress across the huge continent.

On migration swallows tend to fly quite low and are thus liable to be affected by dust storms over Africa and the Arabian and Gobi deserts. They usually travel in small flocks of about twenty-five to thirty birds, although very large flocks and single birds have both been recorded. Before setting off, they gather in roosts at dusk, frequently in reed-beds such as the one at Minsmere in Suffolk, which often contains 10,000 birds. Maize fields are another frequent site, and on at least one occasion swallows have been seen leaving sand martins' burrows where they had presumably spent the night.

On leaving their overnight roosts, swallows may start the day's migration in huge flocks and split into smaller groups during the day. On 15 September 1979 a huge flock of swallows and martins suddenly arrived at Finchingfield, Essex, in mid-morning and left again *en masse* an hour or so later. At the Ruzizi marshes north of Lake Tanganyika in late February 1952 birds were seen coming into roosts in small parties; numbers built up over three or four days, and then a huge mass of some 16,000 individuals left at sunrise a day or two later. One aspect of swallow behaviour that must be mentioned, although strictly speaking it does not concern migration, is the juvenile birds' habit of dispersing in random directions before their actual departure on migration. These dispersal flights may often take them north, that is in the opposite direction to the migration routes, and are perhaps a kind of training for the long migration flights. This movement of young birds prior to departure often confuses bird-watchers. There is some evidence, however, that young and adult birds fly together in mixed flocks on migration.

*   *   *   *

The effect of the direction of the wind on migrating swallows is not clear, and in fact the evidence we have is rather contradictory. When flying low swallows exhibit a marked reluctance to fly downwind, especially if more than a light breeze is blowing, and they have even been seen to reverse direction in order to avoid doing so. However, radar observations of migrating birds in general have shown that birds flying at higher levels nearly always choose a tailwind. Swallows may be the exception to this since they fly at low levels. One possible reason for their reluctance to flow low downwind may be that turbulent airflows are liable to cause them to stall. If a flying object such as a bird moves too slowly in relation to the airflow around it, it will lose stability and height, both of which are of vital importance when precise and stable flight is required during feeding and landing.

All living creatures are affected to some extent by wear and tear on the outer covering of their bodies. Most mammals change the hair on their coats once or twice a year, and our own skin undergoes a continual, though gradual, process of replacement. Care and maintenance of feathers is a matter of life and death for birds, and it is vital that the moulting process, by which they replace worn feathers, should progress smoothly and at the right time. Most birds moult after breeding has been completed, so that by autumn they have changed their worn and damaged feathers; in a few cases, such as with some water-fowl, the birds moult their feathers simultaneously, and briefly become unable to fly. Since the power of flight is absolutely crucial to swallows, they have another method of moulting . Although they replace their body covering fairly steadily, their flight feathers are shed one or two at a time in strict sequence, so that the corresponding feathers in each wing are lost at the same time. If this did not happen the birds' flight would become unbalanced. This would have disastrous consequences, for as they can only feed on the wing they must maintain speed and manoeuvrability. If migratory birds moulted at the end of the breeding season, they would be greatly hampered during migration. To avoid this difficulty, birds such as the swallow have evolved a delayed moult of flight feathers which takes place when they are in their winter quarters. At this time they are under less pressure, with only their own food to find and no young birds to feed and care for. The juveniles also undergo a moult when they reach their wintering area.

The actual process of moulting is slow in swallows and although it happens at roughly the same time in different regions it is not exactly synchronized. Indeed, the process of obtaining new feathers is so leisurely that a number of birds start their journey north in the spring before their moult is fully complete. As always, the picture is not yet complete, and it has been found, for instance, that in the southern part of their breeding range in Iraq some swallows are moulting their tail feathers while still raising their young.

*   *   *   *

Because swallows dwell mainly in the air they are not suitable for the experiments under aviary conditions that have provided scientists and ornithologists with most of their knowledge about navigation techniques. However, this does not mean that discoveries made with other birds may not also apply to swallows, although since swallows, unlike many migratory birds, fly by day they are unlikely to utilize star patterns as clues. They do use the sun as a compass to give a line of direction, however.

It may be helpful to summarize in brief outline the state of research into methods of navigation which birds may use. Many birds recognize star patterns and follow these as they migrate. Experiments in planetariums have shown that a sudden apparent shift in a star's position will at first confuse a bird but that it will then re-orientate itself to take account of the new star pattern. Since studies using radar have shown that night-flying migrants orientate well even when they are beneath cloud, they must have a back-up navigation system. This may be provided by a sense of magnetic direction. Sophisticated experiments have suggested that at least some species are capable of detecting the earth's magnetic field. Birds are very sensitive to changes in barometric pressure, and although this does not as yet seem to have navigational value it may act as an altimeter, enabling a bird to fly at a steady height at night. At least some birds can detect the polarization of light and are able to use the sun as a reference-point, even if it is behind clouds. However, this ability is not sufficiently precise to act as more than a general directional check. It has long been thought that birds navigate short distances near their home base by recognizing landmarks such as lakes, rivers and hills. However, when in one experiment frosted contact lenses were fitted to racing pigeons, the birds' ability to fly home rapidly was not adversely affected. All in all, although we know a little of what birds can do, we do not know how they do it and how they use the abilities they have developed. The ancient mystery of migration remains a mystery today and may yet be one tomorrow.

We do know that the navigation system is innate and is not learned from other birds. For example, a young cuckoo raised by a non-migratory bird such as a dunnock will still set out on its migration some weeks after the adult cuckoos have left, relying only on its own resources. It is possible that young swallows do follow the lead of older birds, at least in the early stages of their journey, since mixed flocks of adults and juveniles appear to set off together.

On their return from their winter quarters the females do not seem to be quite as faithful to a 'home' area as males, and on occasion may go quite far away. One female ringed as a nestling in September in Warwickshire was trapped as one of a breeding pair in the southern Netherlands the following year; it is tempting to believe that she met her mate either in their winter quarters or on migration. There is some evidence to suggest that the extent to which females move away from the area in which they were raised depends on the density of breeding pairs there.

*   *   *   *

Swallows also return to the winter quarters they have used before. One interesting and rather unusual example of this concerns some two hundred birds that regularly overwintered in Hamamatsu on the island of Honshu, Japan, in the house of a Mr Kawai. They first appeared in autumn 1927, and Mr Kawai fitted wires across the ceiling on which they could roost. When all the birds has come in for the night he would shut the doors, opening them in the morning again to allow them to fly out. Some two thousand individuals were ringed over a period of seven years and some birds were found to have returned each year. At any one time about 30 per cent of the flock had been present the year before or even earlier, although some birds were found in other roosts up to three years after they had left the house. Study of this wintering flock revealed one particularly interesting fact, namely that the birds entered the house when the temperature dropped to 40

Plate 2

The farm at summertime.

degrees Fahrenheit, usually between mid-October and early December. The first birds that arrived each winter were always ringed and had thus been at the roost before, and it seems that these were followed by others, perhaps younger and less experienced. In extremely cold weather some birds would fall to the floor and were then revived by being warmed over the stove. Although in Japan the swallow is normally a summer visitor, since the 1930s small flocks have taken to wintering near Kyoto, roosting together at night in huddled flocks on the roofs of houses and feeding over the lakes in daytime.

*   *   *   *

An interesting footnote to man's interest in swallows was published in *The Zoologist* in 1889. In one issue that year there appeared a lengthy, somewhat fanciful account of the efforts of a certain Monsieur Desbourie of Roubaix, France, to train swallows to replace carrier pigeons. According to the report he succeeded in acclimatizing the birds and keeping them on a special food mixture throughout the winter, even breeding them and then training their young to carry messages. He claimed return speeds in excess of 120 mph, also remarking that their speed and small size made them difficult to shoot. The birds were so tame that they would perch on his shoulders. His claims were investigated by a Captain Degouy of the French Army, but as no more was heard of the scheme it would seem that he was unable to convince the Captain either of his ability to train the birds or of their ability to carry messages. *The Zoologist's* report ends, 'We quote these remarks as likely to be of interest to our readers, but have no faith in the writer's idea that the experimentalist will succeed in his object.' To that one can only say 'Amen'.

LEGEND AND LITERATURE

Over the ages much folklore and legend has gathered round the swallow, no doubt because the bird has always been closely associated with man and his works and is recognized by everyone. The chief reason above all others for the bird's popularity is that it is universally regarded as the herald of spring. In the Mediterranean the ancient Greeks held a festival to honour its arrival, and on the island of Rhodes children would welcome it in song:

> He comes! He comes! who loves to hear
> Soft sunny hours and seasons fair
> The swallow hither comes for rest,
> His sable wing and snowy breast.

Indeed, the swallow's arrival continued to be celebrated in Greece until the early years of this century. Although the ancient Greeks in general regarded the swallow as a propitious bird, they did on occasions view it as an omen of misfortune, as for instance in 334 BC when one built a nest in the tent of Antiochus, the son of Pyrrhus, before he went to fight the Medes. In consequence a disastrous end was forecast for the expedition, a prediction that was fulfilled. Some centuries later, Plutarch tells us that swallows nested under the prow of Cleopatra's flagship before the Battle of Actium, only to be driven away by other birds. This was thought to foretell the disaster that followed. In *Anthony and Cleopatra* Shakespeare took up the same theme:

> Swallows have built
> In Cleopatra's sails their nests: the augurers
> Say they know not, they cannot tell.

The role of the swallow as a prophet appears again in a story of Alexander the Great at the siege of Halicarnassus, When a swallow flew around the commander's bed and eventually landed twittering on his head. When questioned, the augur revealed that this incident meant that a friend would be disloyal but that Alexander would discover his treachery in time.

In Greek mythology the gods frequently took the form of animals and birds to further their ends. Zeus, the king of the gods, disguised himself in many different ways. He appeared as a swan to seduce Leda and on another occasion as a bedraggled cuckoo; when Hera took pity on it and held it to her, Zeus promptly raped her. Swallows are not excluded from these avian manifestations. The goddess Athena turned herself into a swallow and sat twittering on a beam watching the destruction of her suitors; later she flew away up the chimney. Procne and Philomela, daughters of Pandion, were turned by the gods into a nightingale and swallow. When they repeated this legend, the Roman poets reversed roles and made Philomela the nightingale and Procne the swallow. It is their version that has survived, for the name Philomelos is now the specific name for the song thrush and Procne (now spelt Progne) is commemorated in the family name for some of the martins of North America.

In ancient Rome too the swallow was held in great respect. Swallows nesting in a house were thought to bring good fortune which would cease should they desert the nest. The swallow was sacred to the household gods (*penates*), and anyone who injured the bird would incur their wrath. As well as being considered lucky, swallows were also credited with possessing high principles. In his work *On the Characteristics of Animals*, written in about 235 AD, Aelian said of the swallow: 'The mother swallow accustoms her young to the idea of justice by impartial distribution of food, training them to observe the law of equality.'

According to one legend from ancient Egypt, the goddess Isis once took the form of a swallow. Her husband Osiris had been murdered by his brother Set, and the coffin containing his remains was built into a column in the palace at Byblos. The grieving Isis went to Byblos and at night turned into a swallow and fluttered around the column where her husband lay. There is a fair representation of a swallow painted on a wooden coffin made for the pharaoh Seni in about 2000 BC, now on display in the British Museum. Although the bird is painted green it is clearly a swallow, but it is not certain whether it is meant to represent Isis or is merely decoration.

In more recent times, lore relating to the swallow has been more concerned with its arrival and with its

properties as a cure for various ills and misfortunes. To
see the first swallow of the year is an especial omen. In
Bohemia, if a young woman saw a solitary swallow in
spring it meant that she would be married during the
year, but if she saw two together she would stay single.
In some parts of Germany whoever sees the first
swallow of spring must wash his face, or he will
certainly get freckles, whereas in the Carpathian
mountains the swallow's effect is the reverse: on seeing
the swallow you should call out 'Swallow take away
my freckles.' It was the custom in Cornwall to jump in
the air when the first swallow arrived, and in Russia
songs were written to celebrate the return of the
swallows after the long dark winter.

The belief that on 25 March, the feast of the
Annunciation, the swallow flies down from paradise,
bringing warmth to the earth, is found in many
countries. In southern Germany, for instance, it was
believed that the swallows timed their journey so that
they could be present at the celebration. Since the first
swallows reach different countries at considerably
different times, the saints' days with which their
arrival is linked vary. In Mecklenburg they were
expected to make their first appearance on St George's
Day; in Saxony they arrived on Palm Sunday and left
on 14 September, while further south still, in Bergamo
in Italy, they were due on the feast day of St Gregory,
12 March. Other legends from the same part of Italy
suggest that swallows will arrive on St Joseph's Day, 19
March, or two days later, St Benedict's day; should
they be later than the nineteenth the winter weather
will none the less vanish. Although in Westphalia the

arrival of the swallows was not directly connected with a particular saint's day, it was nevertheless considered very important. In the day on which they were expected to return the farmer and his entire family would wait at the gate to welcome the birds and throw the doors of the barn wide open to allow them to enter. Further south, in Hesse, a watchman stationed high on a tower signalled the arrival of the first swallow, whereupon the news was publicly announced by the magistrates.

In parts of Russia it was believed that swallows buried themselves in wells on St Simeon's day (1 September), and in France they were thought to arrive on the feast of the Annunciation and leave on 8th September. In the Caucasus mountains in southern Russia swallows, and indeed all migratory birds were thought to bring sickness with them in springtime. Precautions taken included drinking a glass of wine or a nip of brandy—and no doubt the antidote encouraged belief in the legend!

In Brittany the belief was that swallows would be sure to arrive before Maundy Thursday so as to be present at the celebration of Christ's crucifixion on Good Friday. This legend may be connected with the tradition in several countries, Spain among them, that it was a swallow that tried to remove the crown of thorns from Christ's head as He hung from the Cross. Whilst doing so the bird was pricked, which is the reason for the swallow's red patch on its throat and forehead. In parts of Russia it was thought that swallows tried to remove the nails from the Cross. A Swedish variation of this story relates that the swallow consoled Christ on the Cross with its twittering song; indeed the Swedish name for the bird, *svala*, means to console. In Russia it was thought that as Christ hung on the Cross some sparrows fluttered around chirping 'Jif, Jif' ('he lives, he lives'); this urged the soldiers to further cruelty, while the swallows cried 'Umer, Umer' ('he is dead, he is dead') in an attempt to make them cease their persecution. In Portugal it was believed that the swallow wiped away the blood from Christ's wounds. Another legend tells that one day the Virgin Mary had a fly caught in her eye; a swallow came and brushed it out with its long tail and was blessed for this kind act.

A French legend concerns Christ's encounter with a

swallow and a magpie. As Jesus was resting in a
pleasant wood one day some magpies flew down and
pricked His feet with thorns, whereupon the swallow
came to pull the thorns from His flesh. Our Lord said,
'Ye magpies shall henceforth make your nests on the
top of the tallest trees, while swallows shall build in
safety, sheltered and beloved by those under whose
eaves they dwell.'

In southern Turkey it was believed that when
Noah's ark grounded on Mount Ararat he released
three birds, a dove to symbolize peace, a bald ibis to
represent fertility and a swallow to signify the new era.
A folk rhyme about God's birds says:

> The robin and the wren
> Are God Almighty's cock and hen,
> The martin and the swallow,
> Are the next birds to follow.

From the Austrian Tyrol comes a legend that swallows
helped God to build the sky. In parts of the Middle East
the swallow is believed to be a bird of paradise to whom
the gates of Eden are always open, and in the same part of
the world there are legends that it was a swallow that
helped to reunite Adam and Eve after their expulsion
from the garden of Eden; as a reward the birds are always
welcome in man's home.

In Muslim countries too the swallow is believed to be
a holy bird. In the Koran the story is told of swallows
attacking an army of Abyssinian Christians who were
besieging Mecca. 'And he [Allah] sent against them
birds [swallows] in flocks, claystones did he hurl down
at them.' Although it may seem highly improbable that

a swallow should carry a stone, the confusion may have arisen in translation, as the same word means a smallpox scab, and it may be that the swallows brought infection to the Christian forces.

The belief that the swallow brought the gift of fire to the earth from the gods originated in Asia and eastern Europe. People from the Baltic believed that the devil threw a firebrand after a swallow as it flew away with fire and that the red marks on its head and its forked tail show where it was burnt. Another legend that seeks to account for the forked tail relates that Satan entrusted the sparrow with the task of guarding fire; however, the swallow swooped down and stole it, though the sparrow managed to pluck a few feathers from its tail as it escaped. The Buriat people of Siberia have a legend that tells how Tengri the sky god fired an arrow at a swallow when he discovered it stealing fire and hit the bird's tail, removing the middle feathers. Yet another legend relates that in the garden of Eden the wicked serpent Eblish snapped at the swallow's tail, leaving it forked. According to a Jewish story that connects the swallow with fire, although not with its theft, swallows helped to extinguish the fire in the Temple of Jerusalem by bringing water in their mouths. In Scandinavian mythology, the swallow's red throat is said to have been caused by the thunderbolts the god Thor hurled at his enemies.

Some rather unusual variations in swallow legends come from ancient China. Dragons, it is said, are particularly fond of roasted swallows, so if you have partaken of roasted swallow recently it is most unwise to cross water, in case a dragon should arise from the depths and attack you! The Chinese believed that if a swallow built its nest in your home it would bring you good luck, and special nesting ledges were erected to encourage the birds. When rain was needed, the Chinese threw swallows into the water to attract the attention of the water spirits. The swallow was also thought to have been sent from heaven expressly to found the Shang dynasty, the egg that the dynasty's founder swallowed in order to conceive having been brought by a swallow.

In Japan too the swallow is believed to bring good fortune, and on the day on which the first swallows arrive offerings should be made to the household gods to ensure the fertility of the women of the household.

The Nguni peoples of southern Africa, among which are numbered such tribes as the Zulu, Swazi, Mpondo and Bomvana, all describe swallows as *intaka zomzi*, birds of the home. Birds of the home were sent by the tribes' ancestors to comfort those on earth with the promise of riches to come and to ensure that they did not despair. Birds of the home were on no account to be harried or killed. Although we cannot be certain that these swallows are the European swallows, they do visit that part of Africa in great numbers for several months of the year and also associate closely with man.

In another part of the world very remote from southern Africa, the Arctic, the swallow also features in legend. Some Eskimos believe swallows to be the spirits of children taken while making 'playhouse' igloos near the cliffs. Thereafter the swallows return to make their nests by the rocks, so recalling the childish joy of their previous existence; and children too like to watch the swallows playing with their *iglviaks* (miniature igloos). There is a tradition among some Eskimo peoples that even the wicked and cunning ravens will not molest the nest of a swallow.

*   *   *   *

The swallow makes a number of appearances in rhyme and proverb. Most celebrated of all is 'one swallow does not make a summer'—or, in some versions, 'a spring'—which is found in French, German, Italian, Danish, Spanish and Dutch. In the old Testament, we find in the Book of Jeremiah 'Yea the stork in her heaven knoweth her appointed times, and the turtle dove and the crane and the swallow observe the time of their coming', which certainly seems to imply an early belief in migration. Thomas Carew, wrote of the spring:

> But the warm sun thaws the benumbed earth
> And makes it tender, gives a second birth
> To the dead swallow, wakes in a hollow tree
> The drowsy cuckoo and the humble bee.

In his collection of *Gnomologia*, published in 1732, T. H. Fuller quotes a source of some 150 years before, that somewhat quaintly tells us that 'The snail slides up the tower at last, though the swallow mounteth it sooner.'

The eighteenth-century poet Thomas Gray in his lines in his *First Pastoral*

> When swallows fleet soar high and sport in air
> He told us that the welkin would be clear

reflected the common belief, which does indeed have some truth in it, that swallows fly high in dry weather and low when rain is on the way because small insects on which swallows feed tend to fly lower as humidity increases.

Only a few people, chiefly the Irish and the Scots, stand out from this almost universal goodwill towards the swallow. They believe that the swallow is the devil's bird and has his blood in its veins. This may result from a confusion with swifts. The swift is quite widely believed to be the devil's bird, no doubt because of its almost black appearance and screaming cries; local names for it include devil swallow, devil's bird in Yorkshire and deviling in east Anglia. Although the swift's habit of dashing around villages and towns in flocks emitting high-pitched screams may seem somewhat eerie, it seems rather unfair to associate the bird with evil powers, for it has astonishing powers of flight, sleeping, mating and feeding on the wing. However, with the exception of their aerial life style the resemblance between the birds is slight.

To return to folklore: in France it is believed that if a swallow should fly under a cow's belly the cow's milk will turn to blood. This is echoed in northern England, where it is said that if the eggs are taken from a swallow's nest in a cow byre the cows will give bloody milk and that should a swallow fly beneath your arm paralysis will result. In France the cure for a bewitched cow is first to milk it, and then sprinkle the milk at a crossroads. A strange legend from Ireland again connects the swallow with the devil, suggesting that if a swallow removes one particular hair on your head you will be condemned to eternal damnation. In Yorkshire it was believed that a swallow coming down the chimney foretold the death of a member of the household. Similarly in Norfolk legend has it that an unusually large gathering of swallows around a house foretells a death, for the departing spirit will fly away with the birds. Swallows gathering in autumn on a church roof are thought to be discussing among themselves who will die before they return in the spring. It is also a bad omen if a swallow dies in your

hand, an idea rather like the Suffolk belief that if a robin should die in your hand your handwriting will become very bad. In Russia it was thought that the souls of dead children returned to earth in the guise of swallows and the birds' twittering song was the chatter of the dead children.

There are many mentions in folklore of the swallow's medicinal value. In ancient Assyria they were thought to be able to cure drunkenness and also the bite of a mad dog. A Chinese remedy for ailments of the kidney from Lei Hiao (420–77 AD) is quoted by Edward Armstrong in *The Folklore of Birds* (1958).

> To use dragon's bone, first boil some aromatic herbs. Wash the bone twice in hot water, then reduce to powder and place in bags of thin stuff. Take two young swallows and, after removing their entrails, stuff the bags into the swallows and hang them over a spring. After one night take the bags out of the swallows, remove the powder and mix it with a preparation for strengthening the kidneys. The effect of such a medicine is as if it were divine.

In Greece a preparation of swallows was used as a cure for epilepsy and also for stuttering and other speech impediments. The connection must be that the birds' rapid twittering song sounds like a person with a bad stutter.

*   *   *   *

The magical 'swallow stone' has been the centre of a whole mass of superstition and myth throughout Britain and much of western Europe. Swallow stones are rather like the magic stones said to be possessed by toads, and indeed there is probably common source for these myths. One version holds that swallows know where to find a magic pebble on the beach and that this stone can cure blindness. To obtain the stone, man should blind the nestlings of a pair of swallows, whereupon the female will fly to the beach to search for the magic stone; if a red cloth is placed beneath the nest, the swallow will drop the stone on to it, imagining she is dropping it into a fire, when she has cured her young. In his poem *Evangeline* Longfellow refers to this belief:

> 'Oft in the barns they climbed to the populous nests
> in the rafters,
> Seeking with eager eyes that wondrous stone which
> the swallow
> Brings from the shore of the sea to restore the sight of
> the fledglings;
> Lucky was he who found the stone in the nest of the
> swallow.'

In 1866 Dr J. A. Lebour investigated the belief in Brittany in the existence of swallow stones. He discovered that the owners of the stones lent them for small sums of money to people seeking magical cures. The stones he saw were about $\frac{3}{8}$ by $\frac{1}{4}$ inch, with one flat side and one convex, and he concluded that they were part of the gill-cover of a fish that has been polished. Although they had no curative powers at all, it would be possible, he considered, to place a stone on the eyeball and slide the edge under the eyelid to remove grit or eyelashes. A swallow stone was also said to cure epilepsy and, if placed under the tongue, would bring great eloquence.

It is difficult to account for the origin of the belief that swallows can find a particular stone. Unlike some species of birds, swallows do not ingest small stones and grit to help them grind up hard lumps of food. They collect mud from puddles to build their nests, but never pebbles. Pliny believed that the *chelidonias*, or swallow stone, could be found in the stomach of the eldest of a brood, so long as it was looked for before or on the August full moon. In the Austrian Tyrol it was thought that it would be found in a nest that had been used for seven consecutive years.

One variation of the swallow stone legend suggests that there were three different stones, white, red and green. If you put the white stone in the mouth you would become fair; the red would help you to find favour with the one you love and the green one would ensure that you would never be in peril. *Chelidon* is the ancient Greek word for the swallow, and the word *Chlidonias* is still in use as the scientific name for the family of marsh terns, which are however in no way closely related to swallows; indeed the only re-semblance is that they both possess forked tails. The celandine (*Chelidonium majus*) as its Latin name suggests, is also called the swallow herb. Two reasons can be put forward to explain this connection. First, the celandine generally flowers at about the time the swallows arrive and withers when they depart; second, it was once believed that the celandine could cure eye infections and that parent swallows use the plant to restore the sight of their young if they have been blinded. A variation of this belief comes from Germany, where it was thought that if eggs were taken from a swallow's nest, boiled hard and then replaced the birds would bring celandine to make the eggs soft again. Another legend, sadly untrue, is that if you carry a piece of celandine in your pocket you will never lack for money! In parts of France it was thought that if you wore the heart of a swallow round your neck you would become attractive and your memory would also improve. A gold ring left in a swallow's nest for nine days is also said to make the recipient love the donor.

There are many ways in which swallows were believed to help to cure eye afflictions. An ointment made of the ashes of swallows mixed with honey was 'very good for blear eyes and dimness of sight', and blood taken from beneath the left wing was said to be excellent for the eyes. Nor was the birds medicinal value confined to sight. If one eats a swallow's heart, the memory will improve and ague will be cured. A rather extravagant remedy for epilepsy, calling for one hundred swallows, an ounce of castor oil and white wine is mentioned in Willughby's *Ornithology*, and another, from *Mistress Jane Hussey's Stillroom Book*, published in 1692, gives instructions on 'How to make my Aunt Markham's Swallow Water'.

Take forty or fifty swallows when they are ready to fly, bruise them to pieces in a mortar, feathers and all together, you should put them alive in the mortar. Add to them an ounce of castorum in powder, put all these in a still with white wine vinegar. Distill it as any other water, you may give two or three spoonfuls at a time with sugar. It is very good for the passions of the heart, for the passion of the mother, for the falling sickness, for sudden sound fitts . . . for the dead palsie, for apoplexies, lethargies and any other distemper of the head. It comforteth the brains. . . .

Certainly a remarkable medicine!

Pliny mentions what must be an even older remedy. According to this the head of a swallow which has been feeding in the morning is to be cut off at the full moon, tied in a linen bag and then hung up to dry. Ground up and taken it will prove an excellent remedy for headache.

In Sumatra a cure for childlessness was to release a caged swallow. This must link with Buddhist belief that to release a caged bird brings spiritual enhancement, and it may also be connected with the widely held belief that ill-luck or guilt can be transferred to a bird or animal so that when the 'scapegoat' goes away the bad luck goes with them. In ancient Greece women would trap a swallow smear oil on it and release the bird believing that ill luck would go with it.

Some folktales about swallows are virtually fairy tales. One such story was told throughout the remoter parts of Italy. It concerns a beautiful princess resting one day beside a woodland pool while her husband was hunting nearby. Soon a mysterious negress appeared and asked if she might comb the princess's hair. The princess agreed, but when the negress began she stuck a pin into the princess's head, and the girl was immediately turned into a swallow. Thereupon the negress took the princess's place with the prince. After a short time the swallow contrived to allow the prince to capture her, and then, as he stroked her head, he discovered the pin and removed it, so returning the bird to human form.

Another tale has come to us from the other end of Europe. In the Norse story of Volsung, the hero Sigurd accidentally tasted the blood of Fafnir, whom he had slain while Fafnir had changed himself into a dragon. As soon as Sigurd tasted the blood, he found he could understand the speech of the animals and birds. From the song of a swallow singing in the rafters he learnt of a plot to kill him and thus warned was able to save his life.

*   *   *   *

In Anglo-Saxon times in Britain, the swallow was one of several birds referred to in contemporary poetry. This was often of a semi-religious nature and contained many allegorical allusions. These poems were partly pagan, but, as time passed gradually took on a more Christian aspect. For example 'The Life of St. Gothlac', a poem written during the 8th century, tells of the saint's very close relationship with all the wild creatures. The poem goes on to record how two swallows once entered the hut where St. Gothlac lived and sat upon his shoulders and sang to him 'with great joy'—another illustration of the belief that the swallow was a virtuous bird, in contrast to such birds as the raven and the cuckoo which were generally considered to be evil.

With few exceptions, references to the swallow in English poetry and prose, though somewhat sparse, are almost invariably complimentary, repeatedly speaking of the grace and beauty of the bird. Whilst it is fairly rare to find a derogatory remark there are exceptions, Chaucer in 'The Parlement of Foules' writes that 'The swallow, mortrer of the flyes smale, that maken honey of flowers fresh of hue'.

Short poetic references to the swallow include the famous Home-thoughts from Abroad—'And after April, when May follows, and the whitethroat builds, and all the swallows' of Robert Browning, Gilbert White's— 'To see the swallow sweep the darkening plain, belated to support her infant brood' and Thomas Warton's— 'The swallow for a moment seen, skims in haste the village green'.

There are, to my knowledge, few poems which are solely devoted to the swallow. There is a short piece by Abraham Cowley (1618–1667). It was neither very good poetry nor particularly complimentary to its subject being much concerned with the bird's song, which he describes as 'a tuneless serenade', and then there is Mary Coleridge's 'Come Back to me my Swallow', which ends 'The light was dark without thee, My Bird of April days'.

Despite the few literary references, especially when compared with such birds as the nightingale and the cuckoo, to all true nature lovers the swallow remains, as it has always been, amongst the best known and beloved of birds.

MAIN SOURCES

The main books consulted are as follows:

Armstrong, E. A. *The Folklore of Birds.* London, 1957.

Austin, O. L. & Kuroda, N. *The Birds of Japan.* Cambridge, Mass, 1953.

Bannerman, D. A. *The Birds of the British Isles.* Vol 3. London. 1954.

Bent, A. C. *Life histories of North American Flycatchers, Larks, Swallows and their allies.* U.S. National Museum Bulletin. 179. 1942.

Brown, W. J. *The Gods had wings.* London. 1936.

Chapin, Christina editor. *The Bird-lovers' Book of Verse.* London 1937.

Dementiev, G. P. et al. *Birds of the Soviet Union.* Vol. 6. Moscow. 1954.

Dorson, R. M. *Peasant customs, and savage myths.* London. 1968.

Forster, T. *Observations of the natural history of Swallows.* London. 1817.

Gladstone, H. S. *Birds and the War.* London. 1919.

de Gubernatis. *Zoological mythology.* London. 1872.

Haller, W. *Aus dem leben unserer Rauschschwalben.* Aarau. 1949.

Hare, C. E. *Bird Lore.* London. 1952.

Hosking, E. & Newberry, C. *The Swallow*. London. 1946.

Ingersoll, E. *Birds in Legend, fable and folklore*. London. 1923.

Ingram, Collingwood. *The Migration of the Swallow*. London. 1974.

Kirkman, F. B. *The British Bird Book*. Vol. 2. London. 1911.

Loyd, L. R. W. *Bird facts and fallacies*. London. no date.

Lyuleeva, D. S. *Features of Swallow biology during migration* (In Bird Migrations Editor Bykhovskii). Leningrad. 1971.

Moreau, R. E. *The Palaearctic-African Bird migration systems*. London. 1972.

Pollard, J. *Birds in Greek Life and Myth*. London. 1977.

Schmidt-Koenig, K. *Avian orientation and navigation*. New York & London. 1979.

Sharrock, J. T. R. Compiler *The Atlas of Breeding Birds in Britain and Ireland*. 1976.

Swainson, C., *Provincial names and Folklore of British Birds*. London. 1885.

Swann, H. Kirke. *A dictionary of English and folk-names of British Birds*. London. 1913.

Welty, J. C. *The life of birds*. Philadelphia. 1962.

Wing. L. W. *Natural History of Birds*. New York. 1956.

Witherby, H. F. et al. *The Handbook of British Birds*. Vol. 2. 1938.

The books most useful to those wishing to learn more about the Swallow, are those listed above by Bannerman, Bent, Hare, Collingwood Ingram, Moreau, Schmidt-Koenig, Welty, and above all, Witherby's *Handbook of British Birds*.

The number of references to the Swallow in the periodicals consulted is about 280, but the following are the most important for the general reader.

Adams, L. E. G. *Nest records of the Swallow*. Bird Study. 4:28. 1957.

Broekhuysen, G. J. *The status and movements of the European Swallow in the most southern part of Africa*. Ardea. 52:140. 1965.

Lyuleeva, D. S. *Features of Swallow biology during migration* (In Bird Migrations edited by Bykhovskii, p. 219. 1971.

Mead, C. J. *The winter quarters of British Swallows*. Bird Study. 17:229. 1970.

McGinn, D. B. & Clark, H. *Some measurements of Swallow breeding biology in lowland Scotland*. Bird Study. 25:109. 1979.

Purchon, R. D. et al. *The nesting activities of the Swallow*. Proc. Zoo. Soc. 118:146. 1948

Southern, H. N. *The spring migration of the Swallow over Europe*. British Birds. 32:4. 1938.

Zink, G. *The migrations of European Swallows to Africa from data obtained through ringing in Europe*. Ostrich. Supplement 8:211. 1969.

Because the Swallow has such a wide distribution throughout the world, references appear in a very large number of books and periodicals, those I have quoted are mainly in English, or have an English summary.
The majority have been published in *British Birds* or *Bird Study*.

INDEX